PAINFULLY PRESENT

To

PRESENTLY AT PEACE

H. Ganz

Painfully Present To Presently At Peace

ISBN: 979-8-218-29930-9
Cover by: Lesia T

To Dave and Kevin, who played a pivotal role in my
journey to healing

PAINFULLY PRESENT

INTRO

My dream has always been to share my story with the world. A story of complexity that ranges from ecstasy in love to the depths of grief, abuse, and depression. In the hardships of my life, I always turned to one thing…poetry. The first part of this book is an overview of the many feelings associated with my trauma. The second part is all about the process of healing and finding peace.

In order for you to understand how this all began; I have to go back to 2017 when my parents died. This unexpected loss caused all of my unresolved trauma to rise to the surface. Prior to these events, I was happily married and a mother of 3 children who practiced healthy habits and had an active social life. When the call came that my father died, I can't remember exactly what happened, but I do know that I let out a scream so grand that many of my neighbors ran over. In that moment, I felt a shift in my mind, and I no longer felt like the person I was moments earlier.

Like most mental health issues, it took some time to recognize what was going on with me. Once I did, I was knee deep in depression and suicidal thoughts. These feelings would go on for about 3 years, and I was so present in the pain that I could rarely find any joy or peace. Whenever I experienced a glimpse of happiness, I would become crippled with fear about it ending.

Eventually, after many bad decisions, I decided to start seeing my old therapist and we worked together to process my trauma! After my diagnosis of complex PTSD, I would attend therapy each week, consisting of a DBT group and many sessions of EMDR, which saved my life. These compilations of poems are from the darkest times of my painfully present mind.

I have decided to share some of my writing in the hopes that it will help at least one person to heal or find hope. I hope whatever ails you at this moment will quickly dissipate and you never feel alone. Some of these poems may be triggering, but please know all things in life are temporary, including pain.

TRIGGERED

All aboard the trigger train
Where sadness is the ticket
And first class is the pain
Time to get on this hectic ride
Where reasoning skills will choose to hide

Will it derail? Well, that's up to me
Take some deep breaths and we will see
The view is dark and getting scary
Oh my god I'm feeling weary

Time to hold and embrace the struggle
Have a seat and fasten your buckle
Feeling the pain with an end in sight
Hoping eventually, I'll feel alright

Thoughts are racing and the wheels turn faster
Please God, don't let this be a disaster

ALL FOR NOTHING

All for nothing, that's all life is
Working hard and not amounting to shit
Loving without bounds, yet feeling restrained
Helping with no expectations, yet being blamed

All for nothing is yours to receive
It's never the happy ending that you perceive
It's never the great reward for all you've done
And it's seldom a sorry from anyone

All for nothing is the only way left to feel
Constant disappointment, the only thing that is real
The let down and confusion from day-to-day life
Your ultimate reward being agony and strife

All for nothing is what it's always been
You would think at this point empathy was a sin
But knowing who I am and who'll I continue to be
Is the reason I'm available for you to take advantage of me

THE NOTE

Next to my bedside a pad of paper awaits
For the unfortunate time I meet my fate

Sometimes I wonder what would be said
On a day that would be filled with so much dread

Would a simple *I love you* and *goodbye* suffice
Or should I write my reasons and something nice

Should I apologize for what has been done
Or just remind you of all our fun

Could you accept that I am no longer in pain
Or would my departure leave you in disdain

The words on that paper would forever be
The last image you would have of me

So right now, I don't know what I would say or do
But I hope this letter is something that never comes true

SENSES

Starving for comfort
Ravenous for restraint
Hungry for compassion
Impoverished by pain
Bleeding out all of my being
Despair blinding my reasoning
Consumed by the flood that is my sadness
Spiraling into an overwhelming madness

HIDDEN AWAY

Stitches and band aids and all in between
Hiding my cuts so they won't be seen
Coats and jackets and no skin to bare
Hiding my cuts so no one will stare
Smiles and giggles and all that I mask
Hiding my cuts so no one will ask
Agony and sorrow, just another day
Hiding my cuts not knowing what to say
Hidden and ashamed is where I remain
Until I learn to grasp this pain

RELIEF

I spoke it, I felt it, So I know that it's true
I know that it's something I must really do

I'm not sure the exact reason but I feel it within
Maybe this declaration will allow me to begin

It's here that feeling and I'm not sure that I agree
But the feeling is consuming every ounce of me

It tells me I'm terrible and it's my time to go
My heart says *fuck it,* but my mind says *no*

Which do I trust when both voices compete
Who can I trust to share about my defeat

If I do it, will it matter, will anyone care
If I do it, will anyone choose to be there

So here it goes as I stare at the pills
All that's left to do is take them and be still

So I lay awaiting them to take hold
Because I just can't take a life this cold

Wishing for the pills to rid me of my pain
Imagining a future of no longer feeling insane

I wait and I wait and the sleepier I become
I'm almost at peace, the process almost done

But all of a sudden, I see the brightest light
It has to be heaven, but it doesn't feel right

I hear my loved one's voice asking me to hang on
Unclear of what's happening, am I even gone?

Am I still here in this world that's hurt me so?
Am I still here in the world that won't let me grow?

I am confused, not sure how to feel
Because the stomach pumping is the only thing that's real

I awake the next day with the same internal Pain
But I'm oddly relieved I still remain

I stare at my loved ones whose eyes are filled with tears
Their extreme sadness fills my heart with so much fear

I'm afraid I'll always be broken unable to be fixed
But at the same time at least I know I would've been missed

So I tell them and myself I'm ready to fly
And it's my pain that will eventually die

Because
I was loved
I am loved
And I survived the darkest of days
I was saved
I am safe
And I'm here to stay!

PEACE

This burden that is mine to bare
Is the reason I'm finally able to share
A childhood spent in shame and sorrow
Is often why I can't see a tomorrow
Made to feel never good enough
In moments of weakness, told to be tough

As whips beat me into submission
Engulfed by my own inhibitions
The only thing that ever felt real
Was the pain I wasn't allowed to feel

Why is it I could never cry
Why is it I fail despite how hard I try
Why is it you left me all alone
Why is it you never gave me a loving home

So here I am, an adult afraid to live
Putting on a smile and I give, give, give
Sabotaging my days so I feel no worth
A life filled with agony since my birth
Not able to commit to a healthier me
Because remaining in sorrow is safer to be

A life filled with darkness, yet I still see the light
I need to walk towards it and continue to fight
It's time for me to do what I'm intended to
Fly free my love, and peace will find you

DEPRESSED

I smell so bad
I truly stink
Sitting in my filth
So I can think
I'm overwhelmed
I'm truly crushed
No desire to feel enough
I'm not worthy
I'm not here
Consumed with sorrow, guilt, and fear
I don't know, so here I'll stay
I'll try again another day

MUNCHAUSEN

The smartest person in the room
But no cares
The brightest in the class
But no one cares
The saddest kid at home
But no one cares

I just wish there was a way for them to see
I have an idea, I'll start hurting me

I'll start by sneaking and eating for girth
Not working, they can't see my worth

I'll join a cult and have random interactions
That just left me with angry reactions

I pretend it's my tummy that hurts so
It was a baby that I never wanted to know

I'll marry a man who I can barely understand
Yet act shocked when obedience is a demand

I'll weep, I'll cry, I'll disappear on you
And you'll have no idea what is true

So, it appears that you're about to leave
Oh, the plan I am about to weave

To the hospital I shall go
Where a wicked plan I will sow

My body dismembered and surgeries galore
Without you knowing what I have in store

I'll fall, I'll bleed, and of course demean
But at least your finally on my team

LOSS

What a day and what a feeling
Today's events have me reeling

Feeling the fear and not knowing what to do
Embracing the sorrow of missing you

Sitting in this void, unable to leave
Not allowing myself the chance to grieve

My mind keeps saying that you're still here
My heart keeps longing for you to be near

Truth is you've been gone for quite some time
It's probably why I feel like I should be fine

So as I sit frozen, unable to leave this space
I know when I do, your death I will have to face

The relationship was interesting and like no other
But nothing prepared me to lose my mother

VOICES

Life is a battle that seems impossible to win
Left only with the ability to hear negativity within

It says I am worthless, and I won't amount to shit
Yet another distant voice tells me to never quit

I'll continue to prevail regardless of this negative voice
Trying to remember pain is temporary, and fear is a choice

I've overcome so much turbulence from my past
But this voice reminds me these good times won't last

Although I know these positives to be right
It's the negatives I go to sleep with at night

The positive voice tells me to share my smile
Regardless of this pain that keeps me on trial

This trial resulting of guilty without a doubt
Guilty of sorrow and living without

Living without a parent or anyone who cares
Living with doubt, fear, and despair

However hard the good voice is to hear
The only alternative is staying in sorrow and fear

SURRENDERING

There's a void in my mind
There's a blindness in my sight
There's a silence when I speak
And nothing feels right

The senses are there
But sadness is all that I feel
Please God don't let this be real

Bound by the struggle of this situation
Stunted by my constant irritation
Unable to grasp the reality of what is true
Unable to vocalize or break through to you

I loved you for as long as I could remember
But sadly, our relationship is what I'll surrender

SCARED

My fears have fears
My sadness has despair
My intentions reek of desperation
Just for someone to care

Who would I be if I wasn't constantly scared
Would anyone love me if I didn't care
Would anyone embrace me without a smile on my face
Or would they reject me, like most of the human race

If I wasn't consumed with fear, who could I become
Could I be a joyful person, so loving and fun
Could I be the person who projects her desires
Could I be someone who actually inspires

What would I become if I was less afraid
A person uncaged!
A person who gives zero fucks
A person who has the best of luck
A person who moves the world
A person, not a broken girl

But fear is such a familiar place to run to
If it were gone, not sure what I would do
Maybe one day, I'll be able to see
Maybe one day, I could be the brave me
Maybe one day, maybe someday
But right now…I'm scared

ASHAMED

Overwhelmed and tired seems to be a consistent theme
Drowned out by the daily mundane makes me want to
scream

I can't see a future as I continue to cling to the past
Sitting and worrying that my present will continue to last

Over the curve balls that life continuously throws
Unable to share my burdens, so nobody knows

They don't know my smile is a facade for sadness
They don't know my struggles as I spiral into madness

Alone, afraid, and vulnerable as I could be
Yet hoping and desiring for someone to rescue me.

ALLOW

Do you ever wonder what you could be
Allowing yourself a future to see

If only your dreams could take you that far
Where the sky is the limit, and the goal is the stars.

If only the noise inside could be made silent
Allowing your life to be free and not so violent

If only the agony felt deep within your soul
Was a beacon of light which could help us all

If only your mind didn't sabotage you so
Allowing you to breathe and finally let go

If only the hurt you've had would go away
Letting in the joy that's available each day

If only trauma wasn't a complicated thing
Allowing your heart to harmonize and sing

If only the feeling of being numb would subside
Leaving you open with the inability to hide

If only you could take off the mask you've had on
Allowing you to emerge from the darkness to dawn!

If only you truly knew
What healing could do for you

HATE

This hate engulfs me like a wildfire
Consuming my hopes, dreams, and desire

Not allowing me to see what is really there
Not allowing me to let go or even care

I couldn't care less about the happiness that I feel
Because this resentment is the only thing that's real

I'll never understand why people do what they do
But the hate wouldn't be there if I really knew

I know I'll eventually extinguish this flame.
And they will be the ones left in shame

But in this moment, it burns so hot
And in this moment, it's love I forgot

I forgot that evil is not a curable disease
I forgot that greed cannot be seized

Although the fire grows stronger by the day
I know my pure heart won't allow it to stay!

ENRAGED

Ripped from the heavens
Ripped from the light
Put in darkness
Forced to fight
Filled with fury
Engulfed by rage
Bounded by this fucking cage
No one to help me
No one to care
Endless obstacles
Wounded and bare
Embodied by sorrow
Pleasured by pain
This is a life I cannot maintain

CRIMINAL

As I lay me down to sleep
I never knew you were such a creep

A man who takes whatever he choose
No matter what he has to lose

A man who has no respect
For the purity I have always kept

A man who takes away my choice
Unable to utilize my own voice

I trusted that I could close my eyes
Never expecting you between my thighs

Spent years constantly feeling defeated
Unable to speak of the pain you created

For a man to rape me while I sleep
Is why I lie awake and weep

DRAINED

I'm just so sad
No effort to feel mad
No desire to feel at all
Just sitting in a lull

I'm in a *fuck it* type of mood
Filled with gloom and attitude
I'm in a *don't talk to me*
I'm in a *just let me be*

I just hate this day
I want it to go away
Stop pain and leave me alone
Will anything ever feel like home

I want to feel safe in a space
I'm so tired of feeling like a disgrace
I'm just so fucking sad
And all I want to do is feel glad

#GOALS

The funniest and most outgoing person in the room
Is the same person filled with so much gloom

The happiest and most joyful person in this space
Is the same person who feels like an utter disgrace

Thrown away by so many who have loved me before
Disowned by my favorites, wanting me no more

Forgotten by my friends once they felt complete
Left me feeling broken with the burden of defeat

But I'll continue expanding the room with joy
Lifting up others to the point that I annoy

Complimenting peers and validating their light
Comforting people when their life isn't right

Now if only I could do the same for me
Oh, how freeing my life could be

What I can tell you, is my soul will continue to heal
And maybe one day, completeness I will feel

I've forgiven my dad whose constant abuse was defeating
I've embraced my mom who's parenting was fleeting

Whether it was rape, racism, or the pain yet to be seen
I'm learning to let go of the hurt in between

But what I can't seem to do despite how hard I try
Is to accept that I'm worth it and not ask why

Terrified of joy because I know it will leave
Scared to embrace it so I won't have to grieve

Embraced by the feelings of utter disdain
Feeling comfort in the hurt and the pain

I hope to get there at least that's the goal
Until then, I'll continue to play the role

IT'S YOU AGAIN

Hello again my constant friend
Hello to the beginning to the end
Hello to the fear of you leaving me alone
Hello to you feeling just like home

You have been there all along
You have been there through all my wrong
You have been there constantly
You have been all parts of me

Sad to say you suck the fun from it all
Sad to say you keep me in a lull
Sad to say you're not my friend
Sad to say I don't want it to end

The constant of you is that you hurt me inside
The constant of you is you don't want to hide
The constant of you causes so much harm
The constant of you will never disarm

But here I am wanting to let go
But here I am just saying no
But here I am ready to move on
But here I am wanting you to be gone

So, goodbye to the damage you created
Goodbye to the soul you have defeated
Goodbye to the constant damage you do
Goodbye pain, fuck you!

IGNORED

I talk and I explain until I'm blue in the face
But no one gets it and it's hard to embrace

I scream and holler until I turn red
I get a reaction, but no one gets what I said

I'm not sure how to communicate or what to do
No matter how I say it, it's not getting through

So I shut down and stop speaking all together
Ultimately, it always seems better

I don't understand not listening to what I say
I'm trying to make for a much easier day

My wisdom and strengths are for you to take
So please just take them for goodness sake

THANKS

Thank you for the sunshine you brought into my life
Thank you for saying you wanted me as your wife

Thank you for the gifts you brought into my world
Thank you for making me feel like such a special girl

Thank you for helping me to see who I was
And finally, thank you for breaking my heart just because

Because you hurt me, I learned how to heal
Because you broke me, I learned how to feel

Because you left me, I had to find my way
Because you embarrassed me, I stand taller today

So, thank you for breaking my enormous heart
Because it hurt so much, it allowed me a new start

BEING

Addicted is what you are
Traumatized and filled with scars
Lonely is what you continue to be
Blinded by drugs, unable to see
Scared is the only way you feel
Wishing the truth wasn't real
No one to go to and nowhere to turn
This agony feels like a third-degree burn
Today there's a choice for you to make
Let's hope your choice isn't a mistake

PAINFULLY PRESENT

As I conclude this part of the book
It gives me a chance to take a look

I saw the struggles that consumed me so
I felt the sadness and the extreme lows

I witnessed the rage that consumed my spirit
I heard the desperation and couldn't free it

I realized that pain and the past had left me stuck
Unable to move forward or give a fuck

I learned the most present that I could ever be
Was when I was engulfed in agony

Then I made a choice to let myself feel
Allowed the pain and my inner child to heal

Emerging from the darkness and into light
All though a slow journey, I'm feeling
Alright, alright, alright

PRESENTLY AT PEACE

INTRO

Peace is a word that I never fully understood. I assumed it meant living in constant harmony, but it does not! Being at peace means being present in each moment and allowing yourself to feel and process all emotions in your mind and body. It means being able to sit with your uncomfortable emotions and to celebrate your joyous moments.

In order to achieve my peace, it took years of therapy. It took scheduling workouts daily, including weightlifting, biking, and yoga. Most importantly, it took a daily practice of meditation. Meditation is the key to all healthy habits and being presently at peace. Lastly, I spent as much time as possible outdoors. It's so much easier to be present when you're surrounded by the harmonious sights, sounds, and feelings of nature.

This all sounds so easy and it does become a habit over time. However, the beginning of this journey was a very slow crawl. I assure you that any momentum is always better than staying stagnant! There will be bumps in the road that bring you back to your old thought patterns, and this is not only normal, but it is a part of the process!

I want to thank you for taking the time to engage in the vulnerability that is this book and thank you for being exactly who you are! In this world, we can often feel like we are alone, and I hope you now see that you are not! Life will throw difficult things your way, but you are worth the work that it takes to get to a peaceful place! You are a beautiful soul who deserves to live the most harmonious life! Sending you hugs, love, empathy, peace, and acceptance!

ENDINGS

Oh, my dearest friend
Let me tell you a story about the end…

The end is just the beginning of something new
The end is an emergence of the beautiful you

Letting go of habits that have been so unkind
Allowing your breath to guide and free your mind

Your mind so fragile, so delicate, so deep
Your heart so strong it makes you weep

You, my friend, my kindred spirit of love
Will always be protected from all that's above

Whether the lights from the stars or the warmth of the sun
Your spirit is emerging, and your binds are undone

So, fly free and soar so fucking high
Possibilities are endless with barriers beyond the sky

Farewell to the damaged child with so much pain
Hello to the beautiful human with so much to gain

So now I can promise everything is going to be ok
Because right now is the beginning of your new day

DESERVING

I wonder at times if the life given to me
Is what was truly meant to be

Do I deserve the pain I received
Or the parents who continuously deceived
Do my children deserve their life
Does my husband deserve his wife

A wife, a woman, a human being
From a young age I was stopped from seeing.
Seeing the world as a beautiful thing
Or hearing the harmony as someone sings

But what I know, and I say it proud
With such trauma I'll speak out loud
I'll speak of all the wrong or what can be done
I'll yell from the rooftop if someone is shunned

It's ok to expect more of others
It's ok to want a different mother
But as I wonder what could have been
I take a moment and look within.

I deserve to be celebrated even when I crawl
I'll continue to work towards having it all
So, on the days I'm not completely sure
I'll thank myself for all I endure

RISE

You can't just throw it all away
Even thought it was a bad day
You can't give in to all the temptations
Although you want to numb the sensations
You have been through so much worse
And I promise, your life isn't cursed
You have prevailed in hard terrains
And you have persevered through so much pain
You will succeed in all that you do
So this is a reminder that you'll make it through

LIVING

What is life
What is meaning
What is open
What is ending
What is real
What is pretending

I don't know
Not sure I ever will
Never ending mountains
Majestic rolling hills

So many colors
So many vibrations
So many people
So many exhalations

Just let me be
Just let me live
I want to breathe.
I want to be still

That is life
That is meaning
Life is whatever you are being

THERAPY

My biggest advice to aid in discomfort
Is attend therapy and feel triumphant

EMDR, DBT, and Reiki are just a few
What works is individual to you

The first step is to set up a meeting
Some sessions may feel defeating

The more you go the stronger you get
Overtime you'll feel less like shit.

The more you work, the less the tears
This process can take months or years

Being open is all you're required to do
In order to become the best version of you

HEALED

Healing isn't an action that you do
It's something you allow to take ahold of you
It's sitting in the discomfort of the pain
It's rejoicing in the memories that remain
It's accepting that they may have moved on
But knowing in your heart they'll never be gone

NATURE

If a tiger was raised by a rhino
Would it still eat meat
If a bear was raised by a flamingo
Would it only use two feet

If a penguin was raised by a songbird
Would it learn to fly
If a mole was raised by a mountain goat
Would it burrow up high

The truth of nature is that we can't fully know
If it's the nurture that guides us or helps us grow

Or is it nature from all our ancestors before
That proceeds to take us thru the obvious door

The struggle between the two is clearly vast
But in my heart, nurture will always surpass!

NUMBING

I used to have a problem where I couldn't think
The issue was I loved to drink
I liked to indulge until I couldn't
I loved to party until others wouldn't

I loved to drink all my worries away
Then wake up and repeat the very next day
I wasn't addicted, only in denial
This pattern went on for quite awhile

Then one day, I looked into the mirror
And realized I couldn't see her
I didn't see the beauty who had so many dreams
I didn't see the women who made others beam

So I took a breath and put down the drink
And overtime I began to think
I thought about the future once again
I thought about my blessings and all my friends

I accepted the complexity that was currently my life
I went to therapy to help with the strife
I stopped running from all of my pride
And now I sit here with joy inside

MOTHER

You never were a grandma
You were just mother
An amazing and hilarious soul
That provided for us all

You made the dark days bright
And you taught me how to fight
The wisdom you shared was prolific
And your hugs were so terrific

Your smile and grin whenever I would stumble
Is also the reason I stay so humble
There is always you in what I do
Oh mother, I'm so grateful for you.

EMBRACE

As I hear the cardinals sing
It reminds me of all the things

The time you assured me it was alright
Or when you called to check in at night

The moments you held me when I was frightened
Or sat with me as my emotions heightened

The playful gestures and all the TV shows
The homework answers you always seemed to know

I never gave you the credit you deserved
Only remembering how often you got on my nerves

But looking back, you did the best that you knew how
I should have embraced you then, but I'll do it now

WORTHY

You're worth so much more than they taught you to be
You deserve a life where your mind is free
You deserve to have all your dreams come true
You deserve to be the best and most authentic you

What you deserve and what you will get
Will only happen if you never quit
Never quit doing life's work
Then, my love, you will find your worth

BREATHE

Here's what I can say about sadness
It feels like a bit of madness
Reality slowly starting to slip away
Consumed with irrationally throughout the day
Wondering who and what you really are
Your thoughts are hazy, and you feel afar

So as madness hits, what can you actually do
Embrace that shit and let it take ahold of you
Feel the pains and all the sufferance
Be the moment and feel the abundance

That pain will lift, and joy will come
The cycle repeats and you'll never be done
But in all of the emotions and all of the tough
You get to breathe and that's enough

LESSONS

There are the friends I no longer have
The ones with so many memories and laughs
The time spent together was as it should be
The time spent with one another only helped me

Some ended great and some were a hot mess
But with each relationship, I have been blessed

So thanks for the friends who continuously lied
Thanks to the friends who never tried
Thanks to the friends where we grew apart
And thanks to the friends who broke my heart.

Because of you and all that occurred
I know who I am and what I deserve

TRIUMPH

The last few weeks have been overwhelming as can be
But I didn't let it get the best of me
Did I cry, oh my gosh yes!
But I also continued to do my best
Did I get frustrated, oh for sure!
But I also continued to endure

The solution to any bad day or week
Is to allow yourself a moment to seek
Seek out comfort and know your worth
And no matter what, don't diminish what hurts
Everything ends in order for something new to begin
So I'm sending you the warmest hug, my friend!

LOVED

In this moment
In this time
I know we don't feel fine
And that's ok
Cry it out
Fucking scream
Experience everything
Love your soul
Love your spirit
Take the time to embrace it
You're amazing
You're so special
Your presence is so essential

SOULMATE

At times I wonder what I would have been
If the universe never brought me him

Would I be as loving or carefree
If he didn't accept all aspects of me
Would I have worked towards my goals
If he didn't pick me up from all the falls
Would I have been such a loving mother
If he didn't always put me before others

I'm just grateful I'll never have to know
As our love and compassion continue to grow
I'm so grateful for him choosing me
So I can become what I'm meant to be

SEEN

Pouring
Roaring
Heavily storming
Dismay
Discomfort
All things boring
Sadness
Guilt
Sorrow and joy
All the things I enjoy
Hope
Pride
And all in between
Taking some time for emotions to be seen

DREAMS

This world needs to be created, so I can heal too
This world is essential, and it's what I must do

There may always be hunger
There may always be disdain
There may always be starvation
But we all can heal from pain

I want to make a movie where the victim becomes the hero
I want to make a show where we root for the weirdo
I want to make a life that is so fucking grand
I want to make a movement and tell them where I stand

Standing up for what matters, despite what it may cost
Standing up for equality for those who have lost
Standing up for compassion, where hate is never allowed
Standing all together instead of alone in a crowd

A rebirth of humanity is what we truly need
A rebirth of love will set us free
My dreams are so magical and will change the world
But nothing happens without action, so get at it girl

PROUD

Today was such a beautiful occasion
One comprised of a standing ovation
The lights shined bright as I stood in my success
The laughter was loud, and I felt truly blessed

The struggle was rough and yet here I stood
I finally turned this darkness into good
So good job me and what I continue to do
Look at where all this pain has got me to

TIME

I often dream about the time
When the dishwasher will no longer be full
No one to clean up after
And hands no longer juggling it all

I often think about the shoes
That are always in my way
Then I take a moment to remember
They won't be around one day

I often think about the times
When they drove me up the wall
One day, those moments won't matter
As time takes its toll

One day, someday, more than likely soon
They will grow up and move out of their room

They will leave us, so they can explore the world
And we will be so proud, but miss our little girls
So, until then I'll embrace all the mess and tears
Because ultimately these days turn into years

PARENTS

Sometimes my favorite thing to do is just stare
Looking over the crib with absolutely no care
Watching your chest rise up and down
Listening to your breath is the most beautiful sound
Observing your little hands and the blanket that they grasp
Overwhelmed with joy, wishing this moment to last

But then the thief of time takes that moment away
But provides me many more
Over the years, weeks, and days
Time is priceless, but it is never free
So I embrace all the moments of you and me

ME

I write to live
I breathe to prosper
I rest to elevate
I read to wonder
I see to feel
I feel to see
I love to love
And that is me

TRUTH

Hello, how are you
Now ask yourself if that is true
How you answer, is it for real
Or is it about how the recipient feels

Can you be open about your day
Or do you monitor what you say
Either way, I hope you know what's true
And that is, you're perfect, just as you!

CALM

The warmth on my back
The breeze in my hair
The contentment and peace
That is finally there

The sound of the ocean
The calm of the waves
The endless devotion to the road I will pave

The sea, the sky, the ocean, the air
Once again, I can finally care

PRESENTLY AT PEACE

Peace is a method of going within
Peace is where you should always begin
It's an action, a thought, and a desire
It's a moment where you brain and heart conspire
It's a movement that truly comes in phases
It's a constant of unrelenting praises
It's a deliberate vision of seeing the better
It's the acceptance of the hardest endeavor
It's a practice that you must work on each day
And ultimately, peace will find its way

AUTHOR BIO

H. Ganz is a kindhearted, empathetic and spiritual woman who thrives on helping others and giving back to her family, friends and community. She has been a poet most of her life, and it started during the darker and more traumatic experiences of her childhood. In fact, it was her poetry that gave her the strength to persevere during these difficult times. She continues to write poetry for therapeutic and self-healing purposes to this day.

H. Ganz has been happily married for more than a decade and lives in the Midwest with her two beautiful daughters. After years of therapy, followed by a few wellness and poetry retreats, she made the decision to share her poetry with the world. She has made it her mission to help others who have directly or indirectly struggled with trauma and mental health issues. She hopes this book raises awareness, promotes healing and helps others find peace on the other side of their pain.